Achoo!

Sing Along

Tune:
The Farmer in the Dell

Jo Cleland

Rourke
Educational Media

rourkeeducationalmedia.com

Teacher Notes available at
rem4teachers.com

www.rourkeeducationalmedia.com

PHOTO CREDITS: Cover: © Serhiy Kobyakov; Title Page: © Imgorthand; Page 3, 6, 12: © Imgorthand; Page 4: © bjdlzx; Page 5: © andipantz; Page 7: © woraput chawalitphon; Page 8: © Stefanie Timmermann; Page 9: © Chris Fertnig; Page 10: © Arthur Carlo Franco; Page 11: © drbimages; Page 13: © onebluelight; Page 14: © Kim Gunkel; Page 15: © Photoeuphoria; Page 16: © Luis Pedrosa; Page 17: © sack; Page 18: © Jarenwicklund; Page 19: © Rosemarie Gearhart; Page 20: © Sadeugra; Page 21: © Damir Cudic

Editor: Precious McKenzie

Cover and Page design by Tara Raymo

Library of Congress PCN Data

Achoo! / Jo Cleland.
(Sing and Read, Healthy Habits)
ISBN 978-1-61810-081-8 (hard cover)
ISBN 978-1-61810-214-0 (soft cover)
Library of Congress Control Number: 2011944390

Rourke Educational Media
Printed in the United States of America,
North Mankato, Minnesota

rourkeeducationalmedia.com
customerservice@rourkeeducationalmedia.com • PO Box 643328 Vero Beach, Florida 32964

Achoo! Achoo!
I know it's true.

3

A **sneeze spreads germs**.

What should I do?

Achoo! Achoo!
What should I do?

I sneeze into my **elbow**,
keeping germs from you.

Achoo! Achoo!
What should I do?

I sneeze into a **tissue**,
keeping germs from you.

Achoo! Achoo!
What should I do?

14

When I sneeze I **wash** my hands.
That's what I do.

A sneeze spreads germs everywhere.

I'll be good to show how much I care.

Achoo! Achoo!

I **promise** you,

I'll never, never, never
give my germs to you!

Glossary

elbow (EL- boh): joint that connects the lower to upper parts of your arm

germs (JURMZ): little organisms that can make you sick

promise (PROM-iss): to say you will do something for sure

sneeze (SNEEZ): a reflex that blows air out of your nose

spreads (SPREDZ): moves far

tissue (tish-oo): soft paper used to wipe your nose

wash (wosh): clean with soap and water

Song Lyrics

Achoo!

Tune: The Farmer in the Dell

Achoo! Achoo!
I know it's true.
A sneeze spreads germs.
What should I do?

Achoo! Achoo!
What should I do?
I sneeze into my elbow,
keeping germs from you.

Achoo! Achoo!
What should I do?
I sneeze into a tissue,
keeping germs from you.

Achoo! Achoo!
What should I do?
When I sneeze I wash my hands.
That's what I do.

Achoo! Achoo!
A sneeze spreads
germs everywhere.
I'll be good to show I care.

Achoo! Achoo!
I promise you,
I'll never, never, never
give my germs to you!

Index

Websites

www.miniclip.com/games/sneeze/en/

http://kidsactivitiesblog.com/preschool-learning-activites/learning-themes/germs/

http://kidshealth.org/kid/talk/qa/germs.html

About the Author

Jo Cleland enjoys writing books, composing songs, and making games. She loves to read, sing, and play games with children.

Ask The Author!
www.rem4students.com